THE 12 BIGGEST BREAKTHROUGHS IN SPORTS TECHNOLOGY

by Janet Slingerland

12 STORY LIBRARY

www.12StoryLibrary.com

12-Story Library is an imprint of Bookstaves.

Photographs ©: petrelos/iStockphoto, cover, 1; Jacob Lund/Shutterstock.com, 4; Étienne-Jules Marey/PD, 5; Everett Historical/Shutterstock.com, 6; Chris Williams/Icon Sportswire 007/Chris Williams/Icon Sportswire/Newscom, 7; Wellcome Images/CC4.0, 8; Internet Archive Book Images/CC, 9; Nejron Photo/Shutterstock.com, 9; Illustrated London News/PD, 10; William Notman & Son/PD, 11; Aspen Photo/Shutterstock.com, 11; Sandstein/CC3.0, 12; Ververidis Vasilis/Shutterstock.com, 13; Natursports/Shutterstock.com, 13; Natalie Leduc/CC4.0, 14; Vova Shevchuk/Shutterstock.com, 15; Chris Pizzello/Associated Press, 16; Aspen Photo/Shutterstock.com, 17; Roger Bacon/PD, 18; Pavel L Photo and Video/Shutterstock.com, 18; Roman Mikhailiuk/Shutterstock.com, 19; Chris Allan/Shutterstock.com, 20; Mitch Gunn/Shutterstock.com, 21; Global Media Sharing/Afaqs/CC2.0, 21; action sports/Shutterstock.com, 22; Oskar SCHULER/Shutterstock.com, 23; wavebreakmedia/Shutterstock.com, 24; karelnoppe/Shutterstock.com, 25; CC2.0, 26; Joseph Sohm/Shutterstock.com, 27; Albert Meyer/PD, 28; Marie-Lan Nguyen/CC3.0, 29

ISBN
978-1-63235-587-4 (hardcover)
978-1-63235-641-3 (paperback)
978-1-63235-701-4 (ebook)

Library of Congress Control Number: 2018947112

Printed in the United States of America
Mankato, MN
July 2018

12 STORY LIBRARY

Access free, up-to-date content on this topic plus a full digital version of this book. Scan the QR code on page 31 or use your school's login at 12StoryLibrary.com.

Table of Contents

1

Motion Capture Looks at Human Movement

A scientist places markers on an athlete's body. The markers look like small disks or marbles. They mark joints and other key body parts. The athlete goes through their motions. Special cameras capture their body movements. Computer software re-creates the athlete as a figure on a screen. This is motion capture.

Scientists called biomechanists study these figures. They look for ways athletes can change the ways they move. These changes may improve performance. They may prevent injury. Usually, they do both.

Motion capture started in the late 1800s. Étienne-Jules Marey was a French scientist. He was also a chronophotographer. This is a person who captures movement in still pictures. Marey went one step further. He captured all the motions

The movement of pole vaulting, photographed by Étienne-Jules Marey.

in one move, like jumping, on a single picture. He designed a special high-speed camera to do this. He was also the first scientist to use markers. He placed reflective strips on a person wearing a black suit. This helped him track the movement of joints and bones.

12

Images per second Marey's camera captured.

- Scientists first started capturing human motion in the 1800s.
- Early motion capture studied general movement.
- Motion capture helps athletes train better, faster, and with less injury.

Marey's work helped scientists understand how the human body moved in general. Now scientists can look at an individual athlete's movements. They help athletes learn faster and perform better.

Motion capture is moving into a new era. It is being applied to just about every sport. It is no longer used only by elite athletes. Recreational athletes can see and improve their golf swing, baseball pitch, or other movement.

2

Helmets Evolve and Protect

A player in the 1893 Army-Navy football game wore the first football helmet. His shoemaker made a hat with earflaps. The material was moleskin, a heavy cotton fabric.

Other players wore similar soft leather helmets during the early 1900s. In the 1920s, hardened leather helmets added some protection. The newer helmets were rounded. This helped direct blows away from the head.

In 1939, John T. Riddell invented the plastic football helmet. He added a chin strap and face mask. In the 1940s, the NFL (National Football League) started making players wear helmets. The helmets had flaws, though. The plastic broke easily. The pieces were sharp and could cause injury. Before long, helmets used better materials. They also had padding. Metal bars helped protect the face.

In the 1970s, helmets had full face masks and thick foam padding. Other

Football players wearing hardened leather helmets in 1920.

The Vicis Zero1 ranked highest for safety in 2018.

sports started making their players wear helmets, too.

NFL quarterbacks started wearing radio receivers inside their helmets in 1995. This let them hear the coaches call plays. It helped speed up the game.

Helmets protect against skull fractures and face injuries. They are evolving to prevent concussions, too. A concussion is a type of brain injury caused by blows to the head. Its effects can linger for years.

TURNING HITS INTO ART

In the 1960s, a puck hit NHL (National Hockey League) goalie Gerry Cheevers's face mask. Cheevers retreated to the bench. Before returning to the ice, Cheevers drew stitches where the puck had hit. He went on to add a stitch each time a puck hit his mask. Today, many athletes have works of art painted on their helmets.

3

Weight in pounds (1.4 kg) of an average NFL helmet in the 1980s.

- Originally, helmets were made of leather and canvas.
- The first plastic helmet was created in 1939.
- Helmets protect athletes from head and face injuries.

3 Special Equipment Helps Athletes Perform Better

Every year, athletes seem to get stronger, faster, and better. Much of this is thanks to exercise or sports science. Sports science is a wide-reaching field. It includes biomechanics. This is the study of ways the human body moves. It includes exercise physiology. This is the study of how the human body changes during exercise. There are other sciences as well. Some date back to ancient times.

Exercise science got a huge boost around 1900. A scientist named August Krogh studied respiration. He looked at what living things breathed in. Then he looked at what they breathed out. He designed special equipment to catch the gases being exchanged. This let him measure what was in them.

August Krogh in 1926.

Ergometers are much more advanced today.

20

Seconds it took Krogh's ergometer to record a weight loss of 1 gram (0.002 lb).

- Exercise science studies how exercise changes the human body.
- August Krogh designed special equipment for this study.
- Exercise science equipment has helped athletes generally and individually.

Krogh didn't stop there. He also studied how a body changes during exercise. For this, he built an ergometer. This is a stationary bicycle that measures how much energy is spent during the exercise. Krogh's ergometer was hung from a ceiling so it could measure even the smallest changes in weight.

Scientists are still studying how athletes move and how their bodies change. They have equipment that can measure all different aspects of an athlete's body. They still use equipment that looks a lot like what Krogh designed.

What is learned from this equipment has a broad reach. People know what they need to do to live healthy lifestyles. Sports equipment makers can design better equipment for each sport. Individual athletes can use the measurements to tailor their training.

4 Human-Made Ice Brings Ice Sports to Warm Weather

In order to ice skate, you need ice. For centuries, this meant you could only skate in winter. This changed in 1876. The first refrigerated ice rink opened in London. The rink had layers of concrete, earth, and boards. Copper pipes ran along the surface. A chemical mixture ran through the pipes. The chemicals cooled and froze water poured on top.

Modern rinks follow the same principles. A rink starts with a layer of concrete or sand. Pipes run through this surface. Coolant pumped through the pipes cools water sprayed on the surface. Paint applied to the ice defines the playing area. This marks the ice for sports like curling, ice hockey, or speed skating. More water is sprayed on top. This makes a thick, smooth layer of ice to play on.

Over the years, refrigeration technology has improved. It is now more efficient. It is also cheaper.

The interior of the London Glaciarium in 1876.

Indoor hockey in Montreal, Canada, 1893.

This gives people in warm climates access to ice sports.

Human-made ice has another benefit. Technicians can control its consistency. They can make the ice warmer or cooler. They can make it textured or smooth. Each ice sport needs the ice to have different qualities. The right ice allows the athletes to perform their best. It also helps them stay safe.

SHAVING TIME WITH ZAMBONI

An ice rink needs frequent care. The ice must be shaved and the shavings removed. The ice must be sprayed with water and squeegeed. This can take many workers over an hour to do. In 1949, Frank Zamboni invented a machine for this. A Zamboni and driver care for ice quickly and easily.

3

Hours needed to change ice temperature at the 2018 PyeongChang Olympics.

- The first refrigerated ice rink opened in 1876.
- Human-made ice makes ice sports possible indoors and in warm climates.
- Different sports require different types of ice.

5 Fully Automatic Timing Determines Winners

A race's winner should be the fastest racer. This can be difficult to determine. What if two racers reach the finish line at the same time? What happens if one racer laps another? What if only one racer can go at a time? Fully automatic timing (FAT) handles issues like these.

A fully automatic time device from 1948.

FAT uses computers to track racers and determine winners. A start signal starts the timing system. An end signal stops it. The finish line captures results within 1/100th or 1/1000th of a second. FAT synchronizes all these elements without human intervention.

FAT evolved over decades. The first automated timing system appeared in 1945. Downhill skiing started using a photoelectric system. Narrow beams of light shone across

10,000
Images per second taken at the finish line of races at the 2016 Rio Olympics.

- Skiing races started using automated timing in 1945.
- FAT times races without human intervention.
- Transponders track racers in events like motorsports races and marathons.

the start and finish lines. The timer started when the racer broke the beam at the start. It stopped when the skier passed through the beam at the finish line.

Transponders changed timing systems in the 1980s. A transponder acts like a radio. It broadcasts an identification signal. FAT tracks these signals. Motorsports races used transponders first. Marathons and triathlons started using them in the 1990s. The small devices can be attached to a shoelace or racing bib. Today all elite racing events use a form of FAT.

ADDING EXCITEMENT WITH TIME

Time can be used for more than deciding the winner. In basketball's early days, teams could hold the ball and stall the game. Fans were bored. Scores were low. In 1954, the NBA (National Basketball Association) introduced the shot clock. A team had 24 seconds to try to score. This added excitement to the game.

6 Snowmaking Machines Help Mother Nature

The skiing at the 2018 PyeongChang Olympics was good. This was not thanks to nature. Bare patches of red earth showed beside the white cross-country trails. Much of the snow came from hundreds of snow cannons.

Snowmaking was discovered by accident. In the 1940s, a research team in Canada was testing what ice crystals in the air do to jet engines. Working in a cold laboratory, they sprayed water into the air. They weren't able to create the icy particles they wanted. Instead, they made snow.

A small company in Connecticut made the first snow machine in 1950. They blew water droplets through a paint nozzle. This turned to snow in cold air. A decade later, another company invented the fan snowmaker. This machine sprayed water in front of a fan.

Snow forms around a particle. This particle is called a seed. The seed can be made from many different materials. Calcium, clay, and dirt are common seeds. When water mist comes in contact with a seed at the right temperature, it forms a snowflake. Snow machines look like

Snowmaking in 1950.

cannons, spewing out large streams of snow.

Olympic skiers aren't the only ones that benefit from snowmaking machines. In fact, small resorts made snow before Olympic snowmakers did. Over the years, resorts have relied more and more on human-made snow. This way, their ski season lasts longer. The conditions are more consistent.

197

Distance in feet (60 m) a snow gun can shoot snow.

- People started making snow in 1950.
- Machines use seed particles and water to make snowflakes.
- Snowmaking machines let people ski even when it doesn't snow.

THINK ABOUT IT

When human-made snow melts, the seed particles remain. These particles could change the surrounding environment during the warm season. Should people be concerned about this?

7

Instant Replay Changes Sports

In 1963, TV viewers tuned in to the annual Army-Navy football game. They saw Army quarterback Rollie Stichweh fake a hand-off and run for a touchdown. Fifteen seconds later, they saw the play again. Instant replay was born.

In 1965, baseball broadcasts started using slow motion. Sports announcers compared their rulings against the referees'.

People thought referees should use instant replay. The technology was expensive, though. It also needed lots of room. The images were captured on tape reels. Replays required multiple tape decks. Each was the size of a refrigerator.

In 1978, the NFL (National Football League) tested instant replay review. It didn't work. Each review took too long. There weren't enough camera

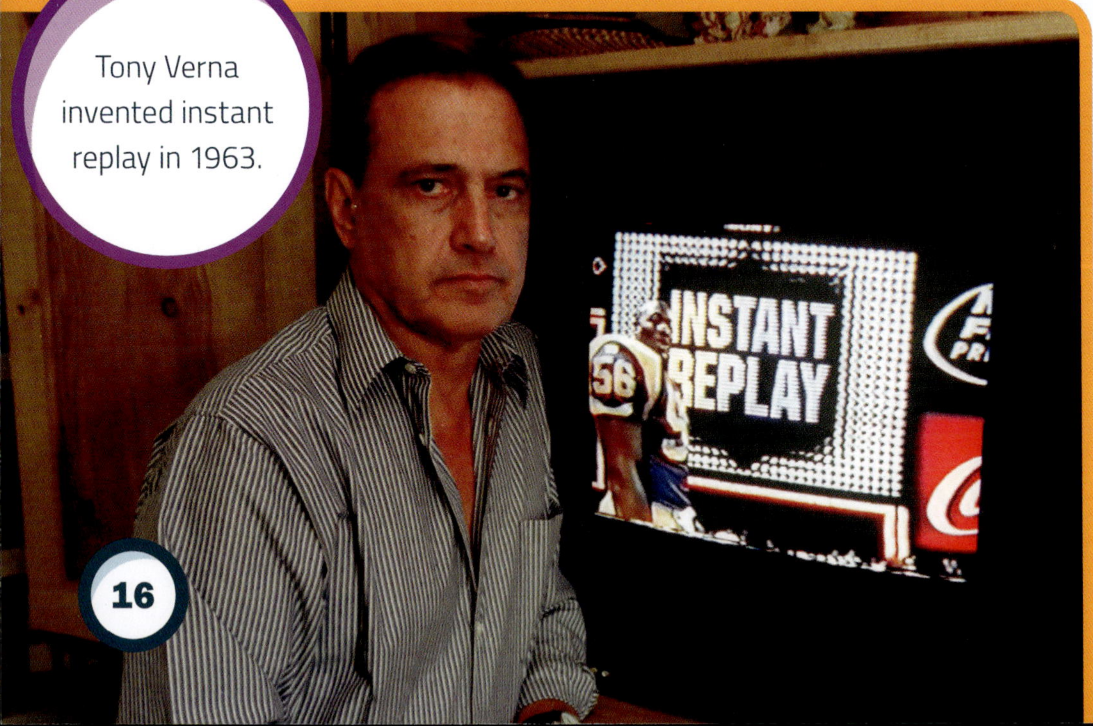

Tony Verna invented instant replay in 1963.

angles. The referees couldn't see well enough on the video.

The NFL tried again in 1985. The next year, NFL referees started using instant replay on some plays. After six years, owners demanded its removal. They disagreed with many of the calls. They felt the process took too long.

Video technology kept improving. In 1991, the NHL (National Hockey League) adopted instant replay review on controversial calls. The NFL added it again in 1999. The NBA (National Basketball Association) started reviewing last-second shots in 2002. In 2008, MLB (Major League Baseball) added video review on some home run calls.

Instant replay has changed training, too. Athletes used to wait until the end of the day to see how they did. Now coaches can capture video on handheld devices. Athletes can watch their performance before they try again. What started as a viewer feature has turned into an invaluable tool for sports.

2:45

Average time (minutes and seconds) it takes to review a play in the NFL.

- The first instant replay was shown on a football broadcast in 1963.
- Instant replay started as a device for viewers only.
- Many sports now use it in training and judging.

8 Carbon Fiber Strengthens Sports

Sports equipment changed forever in 1958. Scientist Roger Bacon discovered a new material. It was much stronger and lighter than steel. The material was carbon fiber. Five years later, carbon fiber could be made in bulk. Although carbon fiber was expensive, Formula 1 car racing saw its potential and started using it.

Carbon fibers are not generally used on their own. They are added to other materials. These are called composite materials.

Composites have properties of the materials they combine. Carbon fibers make a composite stronger. They also add flexibility. They help keep the composite from breaking when it bends. They do all this without adding much weight. These properties benefit sports equipment. A snowboard must flex when an athlete lands after a jump. A hockey stick has to bend during a slap shot.

Carbon fibers are strong, flexible, and light. They keep these

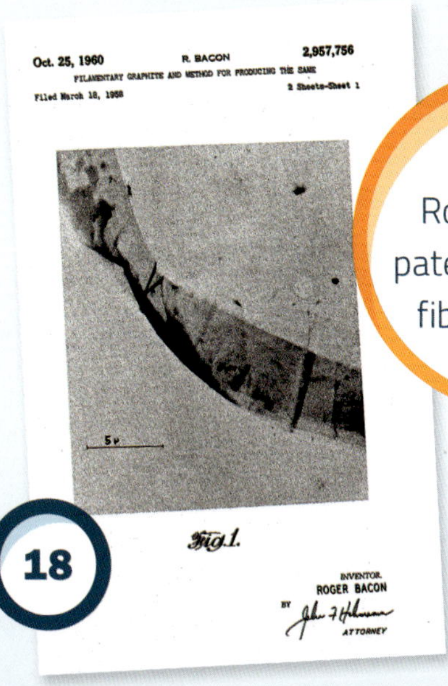

Roger Bacon patented carbon fiber in 1960.

0.0003

Diameter of a carbon fiber, in inches (0.0076 mm).

- Carbon fibers were discovered in 1958.
- They are added to materials to make them stronger and lighter.
- Carbon fibers have improved the quality of sports equipment.

THINK ABOUT IT

The latest innovations can be very expensive. Some people think technology can give wealthy athletes an unfair advantage. They call this "technology doping." What do you think?

properties at a wide range of temperatures. This makes them usable for a wide range of sports. They are common in golf clubs and ski poles. They are used to make tennis rackets and hockey sticks. Bobsleds and bicycles benefit from carbon fibers, too.

Carbon fibers have transformed sports equipment. They can be added just where they're needed. Composites can be made to meet each sport's needs. While this comes at a cost, it is one elite athletes are willing to pay.

The newest carbon fiber bikes weigh less than 15 pounds (6.8 kg).

9 Spandex Transforms Athletic Clothing

A century ago, female athletes wore long skirts. Male athletes wore baggy shorts. The outfits were made from wool or heavy cotton. Then a fiber discovered in 1959 changed athletic clothing forever.

Spandex is a rubbery, human-made thread. It stretches up to 600 times its normal length. It then returns to its original shape. It's not just stretchy. It's also lightweight and strong. It doesn't absorb water or oils.

80

Percent of clothing sold in America in 2011 that contained spandex.

- Spandex was invented in 1959.
- It stretches, then returns to its original shape.
- Spandex clothing helped athletes perform better.

In most of the world, spandex is known as elastane. Lycra is one brand of spandex. Whatever you call it, spandex is used in many modern fabrics. It can be blended with just about any other fiber.

Swimwear started using spandex in the 1960s. These swimsuits hugged the body. This reduced the drag swimmers faced in the water. The new suits absorbed less water. This made them lighter. Swimmers swam faster.

Michael Phelps competing in the 200m freestyle.

Athletes on land discovered spandex, too. In the 1970s, cyclists started wearing formfitting biking shorts. Gymnasts could move more freely in spandex leotards. Sprinters started wearing formfitting outfits, too. Air no longer collected in their clothes. They were able to run faster.

Spandex gave a huge boost to women's athletics. In 1977, the stretchy material was made into the first sports bra. This let all women play sports comfortably. Women started running and playing sports in record numbers.

WHEN CULTURE DRIVES INNOVATION

Some advances in athletic clothing are driven by culture and religion. Many Muslim women wear a hijab, a scarf that covers their head. This has hindered many athletes. In 2018, Nike released a hijab with sports in mind. The material is light and breathable. The shape is designed to stay comfortably in place during exercise.

10 HANS Saves Lives in Motorsports

In car racing, even a low-speed crash can be dangerous. In 1981, Patrick Jacquemart's race car ran into a dirt bank. There wasn't much damage to the car. But Jacquemart was killed. His body was strapped in. His head wasn't. The force of the crash broke the bones at the base of his skull.

This inspired Dr. Bob Hubbard and Jim Downing. They designed a Head and Neck Support (HANS) device. The device has a raised collar. The shoulder belts that strap the driver into the car hold it in place. Tethers anchor the driver's helmet to the collar. This keeps the head and neck in line with the driver's body. This drastically reduces the forces on the head and neck in a crash.

In 1986, Downing was the first driver to wear a HANS device. Four years later, Downing and Hubbard began selling the device. Few drivers bought them.

Development continued throughout the 1990s. Testing showed that the HANS device worked better than airbags. Some racing events started requiring its use.

Around 2000, several NASCAR drivers died from the injury that killed Jacquemart. The most famous was Dale Earnhardt. A crash on the last lap of the 2001 Daytona 500 killed him. The next year, NASCAR required drivers to wear a device like HANS. That year, driver Richie Hearn crashed. The crash was three times worse than Earnhardt's. Hearn was wearing a HANS device. He only broke a foot.

700

Force needed to injure a driver's neck, in pounds (0.32 ton-force).

- Low-speed race car crashes can cause a fatal injury at the base of the skull.
- The HANS device was developed to protect drivers from this injury.
- This device is now required equipment for race car drivers in many series.

Race car driver José María López wearing a HANS device.

11 Wearables Track Athletes' Moves

A professional soccer player runs onto the field. A slight bump shows between their shoulder blades. The player is wearing a performance tracker or wearable.

Wearables have sensors to collect data. They can track an athlete's position. They monitor how fast a player is moving. They note how and when a player speeds up, slows down, and stops. Some track heart rate. Some measure how hard the player is hit. Some even measure which body parts are used most heavily.

Coaches and athletes need to know what the data means. Expert sports scientists develop algorithms to interpret the data. They use their knowledge of how the human body works. They mix this with the demands of specific sports.

Wearables help athletes in many ways. They show how players are using their bodies during games. Coaches develop training programs to support this. Wearables indicate when a player is showing signs of injury. The coach makes the athlete get medical attention. Wearables show which players are working hardest on a team. These players may need to rest.

Fitness trackers aren't reserved for elite athletes. Many people have a FitBit, Garmin, Apple Watch, or other device. These track wearers' steps, sleep, and activity. This helps average people live healthier lives.

1,000

Data points processed every second by a Catapult wearable.

- Wearables collect data about an athlete's body.
- This data is used to develop better training programs.
- Average people use wearables to live a healthier life.

GIVING WEARABLES NEW MEANING

The next wave of wearables will truly be worn on the body. Scientists are working on putting sensors in athletes' clothing. This makes wearing fitness trackers more comfortable. They can provide more and better data, too. Scientists also envision providing instant feedback to athletes. Then athletes could adjust their posture or form during play.

12 Changing the Way People Watch Sports

The 1st and Ten line is a yellow line. Shown on football broadcasts, it indicates the advancing team's goal. Reaching that line earns a first down.

Making this line appear is a technological feat. Football fields are not flat. They are three-dimensional. The middle is usually higher than the sides. Each field is slightly different, too.

2

Technical achievement Emmy awards won by the 1st and Ten system.

- The 1st and Ten line shows the next first down line on football broadcasts.
- Technicians map each field to help the system add this line.
- The line can now be added to shots from moving cameras.

A SkyCam in action.

Technicians use sensors to create a 3-D model of each field. They teach the system how the lines should be drawn. They tell the system what colors are on the field. That way, the computer doesn't draw a line over a player's foot or a referee's back.

The 1st and Ten line debuted in 1998. Viewers have come to expect it. Broadcasters have added other lines, too. One shows the line of scrimmage. This is where the ball is currently at. Another may show where a field goal attempt would be possible. Each line is a different color. They give home viewers a better understanding of what's happening in the game.

This line inspired other on-screen displays. Viewers now see ads behind home plate in baseball broadcasts. They see player stats and pitch counts. They may see vehicle information during racing broadcasts.

In 2017, the 1st and Ten process took a step forward. They started drawing the line on shots taken by the SkyCam. This camera moves around above the field. Previously, the line was drawn on images coming from fixed position cameras.

THINK ABOUT IT

The 1st and Ten line is viewer-only technology. What impact do you think it has had on sports and athletes?

Fact Sheet

- Exercise science started in ancient times. Doctors sought to better understand the human body. They wanted to live better and longer lives. In ancient Rome, a physician named Galen worked with gladiators. He documented human anatomy. He studied how exercise changed gladiators.

- Medical knowledge improved in the 1800s. Doctors started recommending exercise as part of healthy living. In 1854, Amherst College started the first physical education program. Sports became more popular.

- The modern Olympics began in 1896. Countries competed against each other in sporting events. Countries saw beating each other in sports as a political win. They started investing in technology that would help their athletes. Advances in computers, starting in the 1940s, helped this effort.

- In 1976, Australia won just five medals at the Olympics. None were gold. They developed a sports science program to change this. The results were dramatic. Other countries adopted similar programs.

- The first sporting events aired on American TV in 1947. People flocked to buy TVs. They wanted to watch the World Series, boxing, and football, too. The popularity of sports on TV brought in advertising money. Sports became big business. Teams and leagues invested in technology for their players. They wanted to win.
- Continuing advances in computers have driven sports technology. The invention of the microchip in 1959 made handheld computers possible. Solid-state memory, developed in the 1970s, led to even smaller computers. As computers keep getting smaller, faster, and cheaper, innovators keep finding new ways to use them in sports technology.

Glossary

algorithm
Steps followed to finish a computer process or solve a math problem.

bulk
A large quantity of something.

controversial
Causing arguments or disagreements.

drag
A force that makes it difficult for an object to move.

efficient
Able to work with little waste.

fiber
A thin thread.

flex
To bend.

invaluable
Having a value too great to be measured.

lap
When one racer passes another on a track and completes one more lap than the other racer.

particle
A very small piece of something, or a very small amount.

squeegee
To wipe something smooth with a rubber-edge tool; the tool used for that purpose.

tether
A rope, chain, or strap that is used to tie one object to another.

For More Information

Books

Buckley, James. *STEM in Sports: Technology*. Broomall, PA: Mason Crest, 2015.

Slingerland, Janet. *Sports Science and Technology in the Real World*. Minneapolis, MN: Core Library, an Imprint of Abdo, 2017.

Swanson, Jennifer. *Super Gear: Nanotechnology and Sports Team Up*. Watertown, MA: Charlesbridge, 2016.

Index

About the Author

Janet Slingerland was an engineer before she started writing books. She lives in New Jersey with her husband, three children, and a dog.